LET'S TALK ABOUT
WHINING

REVISED FOR EDUCATIONAL USE

By Joy Wilt Berry
Illustrated by John Costanza

 CHILDRENS PRESS, CHICAGO

Let's talk about WHINING.

3

Have you ever
been with anyone
who has been whining
for a long time?

When you are with someone
who keeps on whining,

how do you feel?
what do you think?
what do you do?

7

When you are with
someone who whines:

You may get upset.

You may think it is not fun
to be with that person.

You may decide
you'd rather be somewhere else.

9

It is important to treat others
the way you want to be treated.
If you do not want others
to whine when they are with you,
you must not whine
when you are with them.

ADAM, YOUR WHINING IS DRIVING ME CRAZY! PLEASE STOP IT!

There are many reasons
why you may feel like whining.

You may be asked
to do something
you do not want to do.

You may think whining
will help you get your way.

But whining
only makes things worse.

When you do not get your way,
it might help to
remember you can't have
your own way all the time.

It is not good for you.
It is not fair to others.

When you do not agree with
the adults who care for you,
do not whine.

Try to tell them how you feel.
They may change their minds.

If they do not,
don't keep talking.

That will only upset you,
and it may make them angry.

You may feel like whining
to get attention.

You may need to have
those you care about
spend time with you.

But whining will not get you
the kind of attention
you want or need.

When you want attention,
try to get it in a nice way.

It might help to
  let those you care about
  know you need attention.

If they cannot
spend time with you right away,
plan a time to be together.

Then wait for that time.

19

You may feel like whining
because you are bored.

You may not have
anything to do.

You may want someone
to entertain you.

But whining will not help you
when you are bored.

When you are bored,
it might help to do these things:

Remember it is your job
to keep yourself busy.
It is not up to anyone else
to entertain you.

Talk with the adults
who care for you.
Let them know in a nice way
that you are bored.
Ask them to suggest
things for you to do.

If you do not like
their suggestions,
think of something on your own.

Be sure that what
you decide to do
is all right with them.

23

You may feel like whining
because you are hungry,
or tired, or sick.

When your body needs something,
you may get cranky.
When you are not feeling well,
you may want to whine.

It might help to:

Eat some food
if you are hungry.

Get some rest
if you are tired.

Do what the doctor
or the adults who care for you
tell you to do
when you are sick.

25

You may feel like whining
because it is a habit.

A habit is something
you do so often or for so long,
that you do it without thinking.

You will feel better if you
break the habit of whining.

It might help to:

Ask those around you to help you.

Ask them to tell you
when you are whining.

When someone tells you
you are whining,
stop doing it.

Do this until you do not
whine anymore.

When you whine, those around you
may need to
   ignore you, or
   get away from you.

If the adults who care for you
ignore you,
it does not mean
they do not love you.

They may want you to learn
that whining
is not a good way to get attention.

If they need to walk away from you
or send you away from them,
it does not mean
they do not love you.

They may do this so your whining
does not upset them
or others around you.

29

To be happy, treat others
the way you want to be treated.

Everyone is happier
when no one whines.